PATRONS AND PROTECTORS
Occupations

Art and commentary by
Michael O'Neill McGrath, OSFS

Foreword by Wendy Wright

LTP

LITURGY
TRAINING
PUBLICATIONS

acknowledgments

*In memory of my parents, my favorite saints
in the vast communion. And to Bob Pagliari,
my earthbound patron of arts and letters.*

PATRONS AND PROTECTORS: OCCUPATIONS © 2001
Archdiocese of Chicago: Liturgy Training Publications,
1800 North Hermitage Avenue, Chicago IL 60622-1101;
1-800-933-1800; fax 1-800-933-7094; orders@ltp.org;
www.ltp.org. All rights reserved.

This book was edited by Margaret M. Brennan. Bryan M. Cones
was the production editor. The design is by Anna Manhart,
and the typesetting was done by Karen Mitchell in Berkeley,
Jenson and Mrs Eaves. The book was printed by Worzalla
in Stevens Point, Wisconsin.

Library of Congress Cataloging-in-Publication Data

McGrath, Michael O'Neill.
    Patrons and protectors : occupations / art and
commentary by Michael O'Neill McGrath; foreword by
Wendy Wright.
      p. cm.
    ISBN 1-56854-109-0 (hardcover)
    1. Christian patron saints. 2. Occupations—Religious
aspects—Catholic Church. I.
Title.

BX4656.5 .M25 2001
242'.68—dc21
                               00-052011

PPOC1

contents

foreword

Often we think that the saints did everything perfectly, that they were superhuman, way above the rest of us. But really the saints embody, often in quite ordinary language, dress and culture, the living presence of God among us. They "live Jesus." Karl Rahner has referred to the saints as pioneers, those Christians in each different era and locale who "live into" the fresh, new way that the holiness of Christ is being expressed in the world.

First were the martyrs, those who died under the Roman persecutions and those who died in later centuries all around the globe in witness to the faith. They have been honored not simply because of their courage but because Christians experienced them as being radically connected to God. They formed a spiritual bridge between earth and heaven. They were heroes but were also compassionate intercessors. After the martyrs, the desert ascetics were revered as saints in the early church. They followed Christ by dying to self. They gave up the comforts and the reigning values of ordinary life in order to embrace a disciplined, spare life that could help them become people of simplicity, charity and compassion.

In the early Middle Ages, Christians named as their holy ones not only the great leaders of the expanding church—monastic founders, early bishops, groundbreaking thinkers—but those they saw as wonderworkers. These saints healed the sick, gave sight to the blind, and performed miraculous deeds of all kinds. In the late Middle Ages, Christians focused less on the wonderworking abilities of their new saints but on their virtue. Their lives were measured by the extent to which they manifested qualities that the Christian church deemed exemplary and expressive of the Christian life: faith, hope, charity, prudence, fortitude, temperance and justice.

Later, those who served their neighbors and preached the gospel were recognized as saints. Founders of orders that established hospitals and schools, missionaries to far-off lands, those who cared for orphans and immigrants: These were the saints of the early modern era. More recently, we have held up those men and women who have made a risky option for the poor, those who have challenged oppressive political systems on behalf of the impoverished or who have offered hospitality to the ones society has cast off.

It is natural that Christians should call upon these holy ones not only for inspiration but for companionship, help and protection. Since all the baptized are made one in Christ, everyone in the church is connected in a profound way. On levels that transcend ordinary perception, we sense that the saints are intimately present with us.

Because the saints are both like us and more than us, they can be wonderful friends and companions. They can also be our mentors and patrons in a specific, personal way. If Isidore was a farmer during his earthly life, certainly he must sympathize with those who till the soil. Cecilia, reputed to have sung her love of God, surely must be a friend and advocate for musicians. How blessed we are to have a saint as a companion for the labor that we undertake! These friends and patrons are with us as we ourselves now struggle to "live Jesus."

Mickey McGrath, OSFS, captures in image and word the essence of these saints. His fresh images enchant our imaginations. Dominic stargazes through state-of-the-art astronomical instruments. Helen searches for the cross among the shards of a modern archeological excavation. Always, the Holy Spirit peers out and peeks around the corners of these marvelous pictures, reminding us that those fluttering wings inhabit all the corners of our lives. Brother Mickey's drawings speak tellingly of his own deep intimacy with the saints he adorns with such playful details. They also speak to our own longing to find in the ordinary labor of our lives the joy and hope the saints have found.

Wendy Wright
Professor of Theology
Creighton University

Saint Ann
patron of homemakers

TRADITION TELLS US THAT SAINT ANN, OR HANNAH AS SHE would have been known at that time, was the mother of Mary. As the patron of hearth and home, she has watched over mothers and homemakers for centuries. Because she is the grandmother of Jesus, she and Joachim, her husband, are also the patron saints of grandparents.

In this scene we see Ann (note her sweatshirt!) in quiet contemplation at the kitchen table. It is a sacramental moment in which the humdrum of the ordinary is transformed into an awareness that God is present in the activities of the home. Note that the toaster reverses the norm (the toast is up even though the handle is down).

In the Middle Ages, Ann was designated the patron of cabinetmakers, so in this scene the Holy Spirit is found in the thick of things, nestled in the cupboard. Ann's halo is a crown of refrigerator magnets and notes. The border is the alphabet in primary crayon colors, a reminder that mothers are the first to introduce their children to the world of letters, words and sentences: "In the beginning was the Word, and the Word was with God, and the Word was God."

Grace is hidden in the deep recesses of our cluttered closets and messy high chairs. It breathes life into our memories and abounds in all the comings and goings of our lives. Alongside the busy days and chaos that come with family life, there is, above all else, love, which binds everything together and makes it whole.

Saint Ann's feast is July 26.

Human beings are not like birds, whose instincts tell them how to make just the right nest for their offspring. Homemakers must use their minds to discover how to create a home that will protect, nurture and teach the children who belong there. While each bird hatched in the nest is almost identical to all the other birds in the species, no human child is like any other. The homemaker works to create a place and make the time in which each unique child has a chance to grow and flower into a strong and loving person for whom the world will give thanks.

Making a home that protects children has less to do with locks and bolts than with the loving presence of a homemaker who is aware of the many dangers children face, both of body and soul. The homemaker employs experience and foresight to guard the children from such danger. A true homemaker does not run a fast-food concession. She or he knows that meals shared around the family table not only provide better nutrition but also help the children become part of a family and prepare them for life in the community outside the home.

The homemaker teaches the children of the household not only by direct instruction but by creating the home environment: Tables and chairs are arranged with children in mind; storage cases, cabinets and dressers are provided to encourage children to be independent and orderly. The homemaker is true to this vocation when she or he makes the home's simple, everyday objects speak to the children of their own dignity.

—Tesse Hartigan Donnelly

Saint Barbara
patron of architects

TO PREVENT MEN FROM GAZING AT HIS DAUGHTER'S BEAUTY, Barbara's father, an official of the third-century emperor Maximinus, locked her away in a tower. From there she had a bird's-eye view of the construction site far below, where her father was overseeing the building of a gymnasium.

Her father was devoted to the Roman empire and shunned the new religion, Christianity. One legend says that when her father was away Barbara sneaked down from her prison aerie to talk to a priest who passed by each day. The priest baptized Barbara in the gym's new swimming pool. She persuaded the builders to put three windows in the gym wall, instead of just the two her father had planned, so that she could meditate on the light of the Holy Trinity from her lofty heights. When her father returned home, he was furious about his daughter's conversion as well as the changes in his building design. He took Barbara up on a high hill and beheaded her; then a bolt of lightning instantly struck him!

This is a fascinating legend. As with all good stories, it teaches a truth. We learn that no matter what kind of prisons we find ourselves in, no matter what oppressive forces try to hold us back, our imaginations can help us rise above them.

The traditional image of Saint Barbara shows her holding a tower. Here she designs a tower as the Holy Spirit oversees her work. Barbara's halo is the single piece of colored glass in her modern high-rise studio. Outside are the three windows of her father's gymnasium and a concealed church to show her secret conversion to Christianity.

A motto of modern architecture is the phrase "less is more." We see this in the spare, geometric design and the use of only primary colors in Barbara's dress, office and border.

Saint Barbara's feast is December 4.

As a college student I wanted a liberal arts degree with a practical side. Architecture fit with my creative side and ability to conceptualize space. I was encouraged to have a broad range of experience. While in college I studied and worked in construction as well as learned about design.

This has been a great help to me as an architect. From the beginning I have found architecture to be a collaborative process. I work with clients to give shape and form to their ideas. If I am working on a home, I need to understand what is important to the client's way of life.

In order to execute the design well, I need to work with the contractor and subcontractors, and coordinate all of the trades involved in the building. This means being able to think about six different parts of the building at the same time and how they affect and interact with each other.

An architect must be able to work with the landscape in which the building will be situated. Today it is increasingly necessary to collaborate with the environment. Using straw bale for insulation rather than fiberglass provides increased energy performance. It also protects the ozone layer by using the leftover straw farmers would otherwise burn.

Architecture is a way to express my interest in helping human beings live in harmony with nature, as well as a rewarding profession.

—Janice Vascott

Saint Brigid
patron of nuns

IN THE LATE FIFTH CENTURY, PEOPLE THROUGHOUT IRELAND sought the counsel and comfort of the wise and maternal Brigid. As the head of a monastery in Kildare where hundreds of men and women lived in community, she was adept at knowing when to obey and when to ignore rules in order to bring out the best in an individual. Brigid was famous for healing the sick and performing miracles (such as turning milk into beer!). She delighted in nature and was known to help bridge the gap between the pagans and Christians of her time.

According to tradition, Brigid was ordained a bishop when Saint Mel of Ardagh came to the monastery to consecrate her as abbess. Flustered at being in the presence of this famous church leader, he read the wrong formula and made her a bishop instead.

In prayerful repose, Brigid cradles the Holy Spirit in her shawl of Irish wool. The only source of color and warmth in this uncluttered monastery room comes from the light of the votive candle, the hearth light of the oratory. Above the tabernacle hangs Brigid's Cross, an ornament that graces Irish homes as a sign of hospitality. According to tradition, Brigid wove a cross out of straw for a dying pagan chieftain who asked her to tell him about Jesus. This simple but creative moment won his soul before he died.

White is Brigid's symbolic color because the midwife at Brigid's birth sensed her future importance to the church and bathed her in milk instead of water. (Thus, Brigid is also the patron of dairy workers.) Outside, snow gently falls, emphasizing the interior warmth. The black and white border of this drawing is inspired by traditional Irish-Celtic motifs.

Saint Brigid's feast is February 1.

The most important decision in life is saying "yes" to God's invitation, wherever that invitation may lead. My first "yes" came on a spring day many years ago, when a wise priest asked if I had ever considered becoming a sister. I don't remember exactly how I answered, but I began even then to experience a happiness I have never lost.

A couple of years later, midway through college, I entered the Sisters of Loretto. After my initial novitiate training, life "on the missions" began to unfold: teaching teenagers, falling in love with them, studying for higher degrees in the summers, making lifelong friends. I was never disillusioned with this pattern of work, prayer and living in community with women of various backgrounds. I knew that my vocation was truly a gift from God.

Being a sister has meant finding my place in a long line of happily graced women who have rejoiced in the opportunity to answer their Christian baptismal call in this particular way. We Sisters of Loretto define ourselves as "a dedicated community of faith and service which exists to praise God and minister to people." Our mission is to "work for justice and act for peace because the gospel urges us."

Belonging to this community has given me the strong support and courage to be more daring in speaking and acting against injustice of any kind. This belonging has created an atmosphere of hope in working for renewal and change in keeping with the call of the Second Vatican Council. And belonging to Loretto has blessed me with the challenge and the joy that began long ago when I said, "Yes."

—Sister Mary Luke Tobin, SL

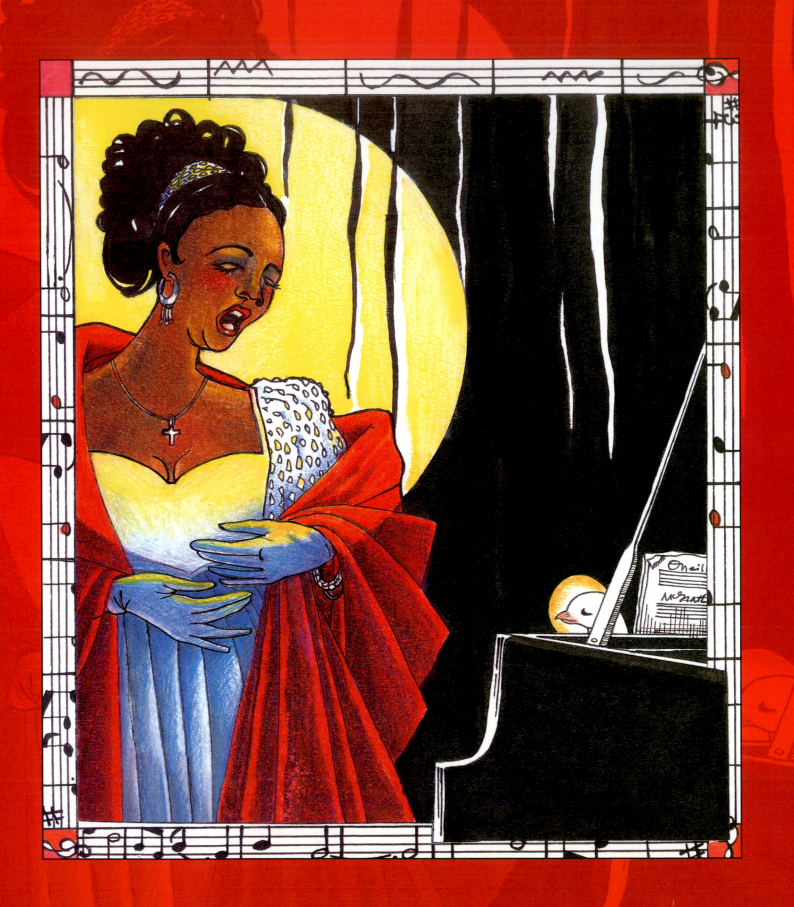

Saint Cecilia
patron of musicians

CECILIA, ONE OF THE MOST POPULAR SAINTS AND MARTYRS IN the early church, has long been a favorite subject for artists. Cecilia was the daughter of noble parents who raised her as a Christian. Her family arranged her marriage to a non-Christian nobleman named Valerian. Cecilia converted both her husband and his brother to Christianity.

All three devoted themselves to good works, and both Valerian and his brother were martyred because of their witness to Christ. Cecilia, too, was sentenced to death. She was shut in a bathroom where her persecutors tried to suffocate her with steam. When she emerged unharmed, she was struck three times in the neck with a sword.

The reason for Cecilia's association with music is unclear. She is reported to have sung hymns during the three days it took her to die. Another story is that Cecilia sang to God so loudly in her heart on her wedding day that she didn't hear the words spoken or the music played. Her early devotees believed she could play any instrument put in front of her.

Through the centuries artists have shown Cecilia playing an organ, harp or lute, often accompanied by a choir of angels. Here, she sings the music of her heart accompanied by the Holy Spirit on piano. It is a private concert, her halo-spotlight highlighting the hush of the song. Cecilia wears a white gown to symbolize her promise of purity to Jesus and a red cape as a sign of her martyrdom. The musical notes in the border are the opening bars of "Amazing Grace," because Cecilia's legend, sketchy as it is, is a poignant reminder that grace and beauty are indeed like sweet sounds that save us and set us free.

Saint Cecilia's feast is November 22.

Bind me—I can still sing—
Banish—my mandolin
Strikes true within—
Slay—and my soul shall rise
Chanting to Paradise—
Still thine.

These lines by Emily Dickinson seem to be a description of Saint Cecilia. They express an emotion and a faith known to us whose lives are immersed in music.

Music composed for the greater glory of God must come from a very personal religious conviction that motivates the composer to try to express belief in God through music. The text is usually biblical, but it may be a poem or myth, or it may simply offer praise for all God's creation.

If the composition is written for soloists and chorus, preparation for a performance becomes a learning experience, one not only musical but psychological and spiritual as well, leading to a deeper understanding of the text. Chorus members often tell me that they have heard a certain biblical text all their lives, but now that it has been set to music they feel and understand it more than ever before. Now it is a part of them.

Music composed for the sake of God's glory must also draw in the audience. If the conductor can create a unity among the soloists, the chorus, the instru-mentalists and the listeners, it is an inspired performance. Then Saint Cecilia is hovering over the entire assemblage.

—Dave Brubeck

Saint Clare
patron of television

Saint Gabriel the Archangel
patron of communications

CLARE WAS BORN INTO A WEALTHY, POWERFUL FAMILY IN ASSISI. She was only 18 years old when her life changed dramatically. After hearing Saint Francis preach a series of lenten sermons, she slipped out of her family home on Palm Sunday evening to find him. With Francis's support and guidance, Clare established a community of women who lived the Franciscan spirit of poverty and prayer. The community soon attracted many other women in spite of its austerity and simplicity. It was Clare's desire that her life reflect Christ's, and for her poverty made that possible.

The Italian word for Clare is *chiara,* "light." So, in a roundabout way, it makes sense that in 1958 Pope Pius XII declared her patron of television, a modern transmitter of light. His reason for doing so, however, is because of a delightful miracle in Clare's life. One Christmas, when she was too weak from illness to attend Midnight Mass, she was able to see the service right on the wall of her tiny cell.

The archangel Gabriel, who carried the word of God to Mary at the annunciation, is the patron of communications, and thus works the control panel while talking to the camera operators. He looks at a wall of television screens in assorted sizes, each one with the image of Clare dressed in Franciscan brown. The monstrance, which Clare once carried along the walls of Assisi to ward off invaders, is her traditional symbol in art.

Saint Clare's feast is August 11.
Saint Gabriel the Archangel's feast is September 29.

When I was in high school, I wrote the music for our senior class song, and everybody sang it at graduation. After that I was sure I'd be a successful songwriter.

Well, I quickly discovered that writing one or two (or three or four) songs doesn't make a person a hit songwriter. In fact, one professional told me, "Write a barrel full of songs; that's the best beginning." Through the years I've written many songs, as well as television scripts, books, and all sorts of things for mass communication, but I've never written one of them without asking for God's help in the ultimate communicating of them. You see, I'm convinced that the space between the television set and the viewer is "holy ground." What we write and/or produce for television, radio, books, the Internet—whatever form of mass communication—can all be mysteriously translated to meet the needs of each person who watches, reads and listens. Once the picture and the words appear on the screen, somehow, in the millisecond it takes to reach the eyes, ears and heart of the viewer, the Holy Spirit, Saint Clare, whoever wishes to intercede, can use what we have offered and turn it into just what each person needs to see and hear.

There have been many times that I've been walking along the street and someone has come up to me and mentioned a certain specific Neighborhood broadcast and said, "You said exactly what I needed to hear that day." I've asked them what it was that they remember I said. They've told me. Later, I've reviewed the videotape of that particular program and could not find those words anywhere. But the viewer (the listener) had heard them—somehow!

The space between the television set and the viewer in need is definitely holy ground. As Joan Chittister, OSB, has written, "God will come to life before us and be reborn in us in unexpected ways day after day throughout our entire lives" (Wisdom Distilled from the Daily).

There has never been a medium of communication that God hasn't been able to use for the good. On that—and that alone—lies the hope for the future of any communications industry. It might be a good idea to write a song about that; call it "Clear Light." We can dedicate it to Saint Clare.

—Fred Rogers

Saint Dominic
patron of astronomers

STARS HAVE BEEN GUIDING LIGHTS FOR NAVIGATORS, PILOTS
and sailors from time immemorial. Pilgrims since the Middle
Ages have followed the "star route" to Santiago de Compostela
in northern Spain. During the days of slavery in the United
States, slaves escaping on the Underground Railroad followed
stars they called the "Drinking Gourd."

Dominic was as renowned for his kindness and humility
as he was for his inspired, skillful preaching and commitment
to study and learning. He founded the Order of Preachers, or
Dominicans, who traveled the highways and byways (probably
following the stars!) to preach the gospel. They sought to
follow the example of the apostles and bring the Good News
to all. Dominic encouraged his friars in the study of theology
but also modeled simple, charitable living. This contrasted with
the custom of many clerics in the Middle Ages, who flaunted
their learning and wealth.

At his baptism, Dominic's mother saw a star over his
head, a heavenly sign that he would grow into a brilliant,
stellar man. In the Renaissance, he was always painted with
that star resting on his forehead.

Dominic, our modern astronomer, wears the black and
white of the Dominican habit. A solar eclipse forms his halo.
Printed on the telescope under his right hand are the letters OP,
the community initials for the Order of Preachers. The lower
border is decorated with the traditional symbols of the planets
in our solar system, while above are the modern, computer-
ized versions. The Holy Spirit flies through the cosmos like
a shooting star, but at the very same moment is present in the
room on the video screen. The God of the macrocosm and
microcosm is with us always.

Saint Dominic's feast is August 8.

*I was born in New York City, and for the first three years
of my life my family lived in a tall apartment building. My
mother says that at night I used to go out on the balcony
and point at the stars. I would ask her what those beautiful
lights were.*

*I chose to become an astronomer because I wanted to
discover beautiful objects in God's creation, and I wanted
to better understand my place within it. I remember that
when I was ten years old, I would lie down on my bed and
stare at the ceiling, wondering: How big is the universe?
Where does it end? Why I am here now? I believe that God
has given me a sense of wonder for a good reason: By learning more about the universe, I can somehow learn something
about God, too.*

*I have been an astronomer for about 15 years now, and
there is always something new to learn and wonder about,
like black holes in the centers of galaxies,
or new planets orbiting distant stars.
Maybe there are other beings that,
just like me, are wondering if anybody
is out there. There is always something
new and wonderful to learn about out
there in space.*

*Now when I look at the stars,
I sometimes still wonder: Dear God,
what are those beautiful lights?*

—Jean Quashnock

Saint Dorothy
patron of florists

SAINT DOROTHY, POPULAR VIRGIN AND MARTYR OF THE EARLY church, is traditionally shown with apples and flowers, the fruits of the garden of paradise. She was martyred during Diocletian's persecution of Christians. As she was led to her execution, a lawyer in the crowd named Theophilus jeered at her to send him fruits and flowers from this heavenly garden she called home. The day after her martyrdom, a messenger knocked on his door with a basket of apples and roses, both out of season at the time. The attached card said, "I am waiting for you in the garden." The man converted, and he too was soon martyred.

Dorothy sits before her shop window. She is portrayed here as a Guatemalan woman because of that culture's beautiful celebrations of flowers and color. Her hair is braided with flowers and ribbons. Flowers are embroidered on her blouse and create a vine around the border. Dorothy meditates on the flowers in her hands: three daisies to symbolize the Holy Trinity and a red rose for martyrdom. Her halo is a wreath of grapevine.

Dorothy's legend reminds us that the garden of paradise has been reopened to us. We too will share in its glory.

Saint Dorothy's feast is February 6.

Tell people you are a florist and they think you spend the day creating beautiful flower arrangements. That is only a small part! The ability to create beautiful arrangements on demand is essential, but much more is required. A flower shop demands hard work: The buckets require daily cleaning and changing; plants must be bought and displayed.

Most important for the florist, however, is the ability to work with people. Florists encounter people at very emotional times. Birthdays, anniversaries and weddings, illness, crisis and death are daily subjects in a flower shop. Whatever the occasion, it is my job to transform my customers' feelings, wishes and tastes into flowers.

Flowers are a large part of celebrations: Christmas, Easter, first communion, confirmation, graduation. For us, holidays often require ten- to fifteen-hour days.

Many flower shops are still family businesses. My parents started our shop over 50 years ago, and 20 years ago I followed in their footsteps. It was hard work, but I had the flexibility to bring my young daughter with me. The shop continues to flourish. It's a great career!

—Therese Maguire Hester

Saint Elizabeth of Hungary
patron of bakers

ELIZABETH, DAUGHTER OF THE KING OF HUNGARY, WAS SENT at the age of four to the court of her future husband, Ludwig, in southern Germany. Ludwig and Elizabeth grew up together as friends and then as spouses. Surrounded by wealth and royalty, Elizabeth was drawn to a life of prayer and service to the poor. Her husband supported her endeavors even against the wishes of his family and the nobility.

Elizabeth used her resources to establish hospitals, hospices and kitchens for the poor all over the land. In time of famine she opened the royal storehouses to them and even delivered bread door to door. While he supported his wife's devotion to the needy, Ludwig feared she would catch leprosy and asked her not to do it. Once he asked to see what she had concealed in her dress. When she opened her cloak, roses fell out instead of the bread she was hiding. Thus, she became patron of bakers!

Elizabeth's halo is a crown of bread. In her arms are the things that bakers create for us to keep body and soul together: chocolate chip cookies for the body and the bread of life for the soul. These same symbols are carried throughout the border. They are what we call "comfort foods." They nourish our sagging spirits and help us create memories of all those who have gone before us, whether it be the sacramental bread of the communion of saints or the cookies fresh out of our grandmother's oven. Saint Elizabeth reminds us that something as ordinary as bread can be turned into something quite extraordinary.

Saint Elizabeth of Hungary's feast is November 17.

Why am I a baker? It's really about the bread.

I grew up eating my mother's bread. She made the sign of the cross as she put it in the oven. She baked it because my father so often extolled his mother's bread. All mothers' breads are sacred.

In school I learned that Jesus made the bread his body, and his body became the bread. I made my first communion, and I became the bread.

I learned to make bread with my mother; then I made it for my mother and for my friends. Then I made bread with my friends to be consecrated at Mass. My life was still about the bread.

A logo of a baker shoving loaves into a hearth invited me to come "make bread." The shop where I work is based on bread. The soups come in bread bowls; the sandwiches and pizza are built on bread; we make croutons and French toast and crisp bread. A cafeteria design makes the place curiously eucharistic. Hungry people line up for bread, and some leave with bread to share.

When my bakery/tearoom is born, bread and sweets of many cultures and seasons, of fasting and feasting, will feed people with memories of their mothers, their homelands and their faith. And it will still really be about the bread.

—Christine Kenny-Sheputis

Saint Frances Xavier Cabrini
patron of hospital administrators

Saints Cosmas and Damian
patrons of surgeons

"FEISTY" BEST DESCRIBES MOTHER CABRINI, OR FRANCES Xavier Cabrini, as she is more formally known. The first canonized American citizen, she was a tiny Italian filled with courage and prodigious energy.

She dreamed of being a missionary in China, but Pope Leo XIII asked her to work with the Italian immigrants of New York City. So in 1889 she and six sisters from the community Mother Cabrini founded, the Missionary Sisters of the Sacred Heart, left for America. Not content to stay put, she crisscrossed North and South America, even crossing the Andes on a mule. She made 31 trips across the ocean despite her fear of water.

During her life Frances opened 67 institutions—hospitals, schools and orphanages—for her sisters to operate. She once said that with God and five pennies she could do anything.

Here, we see her, clipboard in hand, in the hospital hallway. An astute leader and administrator, Mother Cabrini was known to climb high ladders to check on the details of construction and to correct the construction workers when they used vulgar language. Dressed for success in "power colors," she wears a blouse reminiscent of her religious habit, which had a big bow under the chin. Saints Cosmas and Damian, the patrons of surgeons, peer out from the operating room. The elevator door opens to reveal the presence of Holy Spirit.

Saint Frances Xavier Cabrini's feast is November 13.
Saints Cosmas and Damian's feast is September 26.

Each day, hospitals have some of the happiest and saddest moments in people's lives. The birth of a beautiful new baby is a never-forgotten moment in a family's life. Being part of making sure it is a safe and healthy birth, as well as sharing in the family's joy, is a great privilege. I am always happy if the hospital, because it is managed well, can welcome the family for this birth, even if the family cannot afford to pay for the care they receive.

The diagnosis of a serious illness or the death of a loved one is also an important moment. Patients come to the hospital hoping we can restore them to health. They are usually frightened, and it is wonderful to see them not only get better but feel like they were treated as a member of a family. Developing a hospital in which staff are caring and skilled, as well as supportive, to the dying is another way of continuing the healing ministry of Jesus.

Each day I work with so many people who really care about patients and their families, and who treat them with respect whether they are rich or destitute. Many people in the United States today can't afford care, just as in Mother Cabrini's day, and it is important to manage a hospital in such way that we can reach out to them.

I have been involved in health care for 30 years, and a CEO for over 14. It is still wonderful to read the gospel stories of Jesus with the sick. When they say to him, "You can heal me if you want to," he responds, "Of course, I want to." Each day we try to make our hospital a place where we say by our actions and words, "Of course, we want to help you."

—*Sister Carol Keehan, DC*

Saint Francis de Sales
patron of journalists and writers

IT IS EASY TO UNDERSTAND WHY POPE PIUS XI DECLARED IN 1923 that this doctor of the church was patron of journalists and writers. In his lifetime, Francis de Sales wrote over 17,000 letters of spiritual direction to people all over France. In addition, he wrote hundreds of devotional pamphlets and two of the great classics of Christian mystical literature. His *Introduction to the Devout Life* differs from other devotional literature of the time in being addressed to all people, laity as well as clergy. Francis believed we are all called to holiness, whatever our station or work in life.

Francis was appointed bishop of Geneva in 1602, during a period of strong anti-Catholicism in that area. Catholics were not welcome in that part of Switzerland, and Francis ministered to the diocese from his hometown of Annecy, France. From that distance he exerted a moderating and healing influence through his preaching and administration. With his friend, Saint Jane de Chantal, he founded the Sisters of the Visitation.

Francis is up at the midnight hour working by the light of a full moon. Did the patron saint of journalists and writers ever suffer from writer's block? Or perhaps he is striking while the iron is hot, energized by creative inspiration, which doesn't always go to sleep when we want to. People wonder how writers and artists work if they are blocked or just not "in the mood." But creative energy, like prayer, comes from a deeper place.

Francis de Sales asks us how we learn to love. It is by loving! So too with writing—one word at a time. Before we know it, we're writing and loving—beyond the "blocks."

Saint Francis de Sales's feast is January 24.

The author of Matthew's gospel wrote, "Blessed are those who hunger and thirst for righteousness, for they will be filled" (Matthew 5:6). I would like to think my career as a journalist has been one characterized by a hunger and thirst for righteousness, and has been pleasing to God.

Some 35 years ago, as a young college graduate, I volunteered to go to Vietnam. Full of idealism, I decided to work with impoverished war refugees. Moved by their plight, I began recording their stories to send back home. I knew little about writing at the time, but I soon learned what good editors can do to make ordinary writers look extraordinary!

The first article I published appeared in the National Catholic Reporter (NCR) *in the summer of 1966. I stayed in Vietnam through most of the war years, writing for Catholic publications and for* The New York Times *and* Time *magazine. I wrote about people whose lives were being decimated by the conflict—as the Vietnamese put it, about the ants being crushed by the elephants.*

More than a third of a century later, I continue to try to focus my energies as a journalist on the marginalized among us. Their stories need a wide audience. And I continue to write for the NCR, having been its editor for 17 years and now its publisher for three.

Journalism is a noble career. Good journalists try to be objective in their writing. This, however, leaves enormous latitude when it comes to subject matter. I write with purpose. Good journalism, it is said, "tries to comfort the afflicted and afflict the comfortable." The hunger and thirst for righteousness, as I see it, is both a biblical and a professional mandate.

—Thomas C. Fox

Saint Helen
patron of archeologists

CONSTANTINE THE GREAT SENT HIS MOTHER, HELEN, A recently converted Christian, to Palestine to oversee the construction of buildings on holy Christian sites. While there, Helen had a vision that helped her locate Jesus' cross. Following this discovery, she also had churches built in Bethlehem and on the Mount of Olives.

In this drawing, Helen sits in the dark depths of a modern excavation site and contemplates the mystery of the cross. This unique site offers us glimpses of masks, sculptures, paintings and jewels from cultures all around the world. The Holy Spirit sits in the Holy Grail, the cup used by Christ at the Last Supper, which was the most sought-after Christian artifact during the Middle Ages. The border patterns are common decorative motifs from Japan, Korea, Africa, Greece, Egypt and precolonial America. Note Helen's son's name written in Roman lettering!

Saint Ambrose said that Helen worshiped not the wood of the cross but the Savior who hung on it. The spiritual power that comes from being in contact with relics and holy objects points us to God. Archeological discoveries help us understand the past and imagine better what we can no longer see before us.

Saint Helen's feast is August 18.

The 4:00 AM rousting out of bed takes a little getting used to! The dig director bangs cheerfully on the doors, announcing "Boker Tov" ("Good morning" in Hebrew). The sun hasn't yet begun to climb over the highlands, and we archeologists are already in the field, setting up tools for the morning dig in Caesarae Maritima, Israel. As I sift through the ancient pottery we uncovered the day before, I wonder to whom this broken cooking pot belonged and what ancient foodstuff it held—perhaps a delicious meal of bread and vegetables or the spicy fish sauce gar, a favorite of Roman soldiers.

Such are the delights of archeology. We find in the soil of civilizations long past a clue to their cultures and lifestyles, evidence of their tastes, interests, hopes. Pieces of ivory inlay that once decorated a trinket box and bits of jewelry from a necklace are voiceless reminders that others have gone before us, people with names and families, and lives rich in experiences far different from our own.

I came to archeology as a volunteer several years ago. As a teacher of biblical studies, I wanted to better understand how archeology informed the biblical text. What could ancient remains tell me about the times Jesus lived? Like Saint Helen more than 1,500 years before me, I wanted to stand in places made holy by the memory of our ancestors in faith.

—Sister Laurie Brink, OP

Saint Isidore
patron of farmers

ISIDORE, A FARMER AND MAN OF THE EARTH, SAW GOD'S HAND in all of creation. He is said to have loved all animals and was concerned for their well-being. He and his wife, Saint Maria de la Cabeza, lived and ate with the poor, happily sharing what little they had with those in need.

Isidore was a pious man who attended daily Mass and prayed while laboring in the fields. His fellow laborers complained to the landowner that Isidore's prayer life interfered with his work. He was frequently late for work because he stopped at the church for Mass in the morning, and throughout the day would get so distracted by his meditations that he slowed down his production. One day his boss spied on him and discovered Isidore praying under the trees while snow-white oxen guided by angels plowed the fields for him.

Isidore sits on the tailgate of his truck and prays his rosary. A migrant farmworker, he rests his arm on crates of freshly picked lettuce that hide the Holy Spirit. On his head is a straw hat, a fitting halo for such a dignified farmworker. The wooden handle of the shovel rests against the truck at the top but comes forward into our space at the bottom. This distortion of space reminds us that prayer places us in a realm with different laws than our physical world.

Saint Isidore's feast is May 15.

I had never planted a seed in my life until the summer of 1985. I was almost 30 years old. But the experience of working on an organic vegetable farm that year was one of the most satisfying, interesting and important choices I have made in my life. The determination to farm has been a passion that has stayed with me ever since then.

I have not discovered anything else that is nearly as complex and interesting as farming, because good farming is mostly a study of nature and how to work with it. I have grown to love the hope associated with planting, the excitement of harvesting, and the pleasure of going to bed dog-tired. I love to spend the day outdoors, to listen to the songs of birds, to notice the sky and the movements of the seasons. I experience something so profoundly joyful and compelling in my relationship to land that I am tempted to call it an experience of the divine.

I farm because it is work that is absolutely necessary for our survival. I farm because I want to take care of land, to leave it in better condition than I found it—this is also necessary for our survival. I farm because I want a relationship to the world as it is given to us by the Creator: green, fertile and wondrously alive. I farm because it is a daily occasion of awe.

—Jack Jezreel

Saint Joan of Arc
patron of members of the military

Saint Ignatius of Loyola
patron of soldiers

JOAN OF ARC LIVED ONLY UNTIL THE AGE OF 19, BUT SINCE HER death in 1431, she has been an endless source of fascination both in the church and in the world. Artists have painted scenes from her life, and writers and dramatists have turned her story into plays, films and novels.

She was a young peasant who heard voices and had visions that called her to save France from English occupation. She stood up to those who doubted her and followed her calling in the face of abuse and ridicule from both church and civil leaders. She was successful in leading her troops to victory but was later captured by the English. Joan of Arc spent the last months of her life undergoing grueling court trials. She was imprisoned, tortured and sentenced to a gruesome death.

Here Joan is on a rescue mission, helping the victims of a flood, just as the military is asked to do in times of natural disasters. Wearing camouflage battle fatigues and sunglasses, Joan is assisted by Ignatius of Loyola, a soldier himself before he was wounded, in getting an elderly lady to dry land. Lightning bolts break through the camouflage-patterned border as a reminder of Joan's death by burning at the stake. As she was dying, she asked for a crucifix and repeated the name of Jesus, whose peace she sought in the midst of great torment. She was not canonized until 1920.

Saint Joan of Arc's feast is May 30.
Saint Ignatius of Loyola's feast is July 31.

Today, as always, countries war against each other, and men and women are called to the trials of military service. Without their service, their countries would be at the mercy of the aggression and greed of other nations. A desire to contribute to and increase the greatness of a nation leads people today to make the same sacrifices and face the same challenges Joan of Arc embraced. They may not experience divine inspiration, but they do feel called to contribute to something greater than themselves.

Citizens trained in the terrible but necessary art of warfare are often misunderstood. This is no less so today than it was when a 17-year-old girl applied to a prince for the job of general 500 years ago. To some, maintaining a standing military seems contrary to certain important values. The truth, as I have seen it, is that young men and women called to military service challenge themselves to do right. They seek responsibility and grow as much as they are supported by their nation.

Having traveled the world, I can say that we live in a special place. For all of our faults, we enjoy freedoms and a respect for life that make America unique.

—Edward L. Jeep, USMC

Saint John Baptist de la Salle
patron of teachers

JOHN BAPTIST DE LA SALLE, A MAN OF REMARKABLE VISION AND insight, gave up his wealth to follow his dream. He believed that the poor and delinquent deserved a good education as much as the wealthy, a radical belief at his time. His manual, *The Conduct of Schools*, changed the whole approach to elementary education in France and eventually the world. Classes were taught in French instead of Latin, and groups of students learned together in a classroom setting instead of the traditional one-to-one approach.

To further this mission, he founded the Christian Brothers, a religious order dedicated not only to the education of youth but to the training of educators as well. He opened the first teachers' college to prepare young men to teach in small, poor villages throughout France.

Here, Saint John enjoys a quiet moment in his classroom at the end of the day. He pauses from grading tests and marking papers while the Holy Spirit has fun at the blackboard. The border symbols show us the basics of elementary education: reading, writing and arithmetic, gifts that John believed should be shared with all youth. In 1950 Pope Pius XII declared him patron of all school teachers, putting under his protection those who believe that the light and wisdom of God is meant for all, not just a privileged few.

Saint John Baptist de la Salle's feast is April 7.

A few years ago at Mass we sang a song with the words, "When I was little you taught me to read." I found myself weeping with those words; that's what I do, I teach people to read. We had never sung about my job in church before!

Teaching is a great ministry because every year I meet new young people, and I work to give them the gift of literacy. I teach them to love reading and to use it as a tool to enrich their lives and the lives of others. I challenge them to learn about the world, and I teach them to strive for peace.

I hated school when I was a little girl and decided at age seven to become a teacher—and promised myself that I would never let my class be boring! After 27 years in this profession, I am still energized and rejuvenated by the children I teach. I visit their homes and invite their families to share their cultures, their languages, their lives. I get to know the aging grandma who lives with them, or the brand-new baby. We build great trust and love, which helps everyone learn so much better. I treasure the letters that students write to me when they are older, telling me how they turned out!

Teaching is new every day. The various students bring their own knowledge and experiences that enrich us all. My brain spins with ideas, and my heart holds these children dear.

—Theresa Kubasak

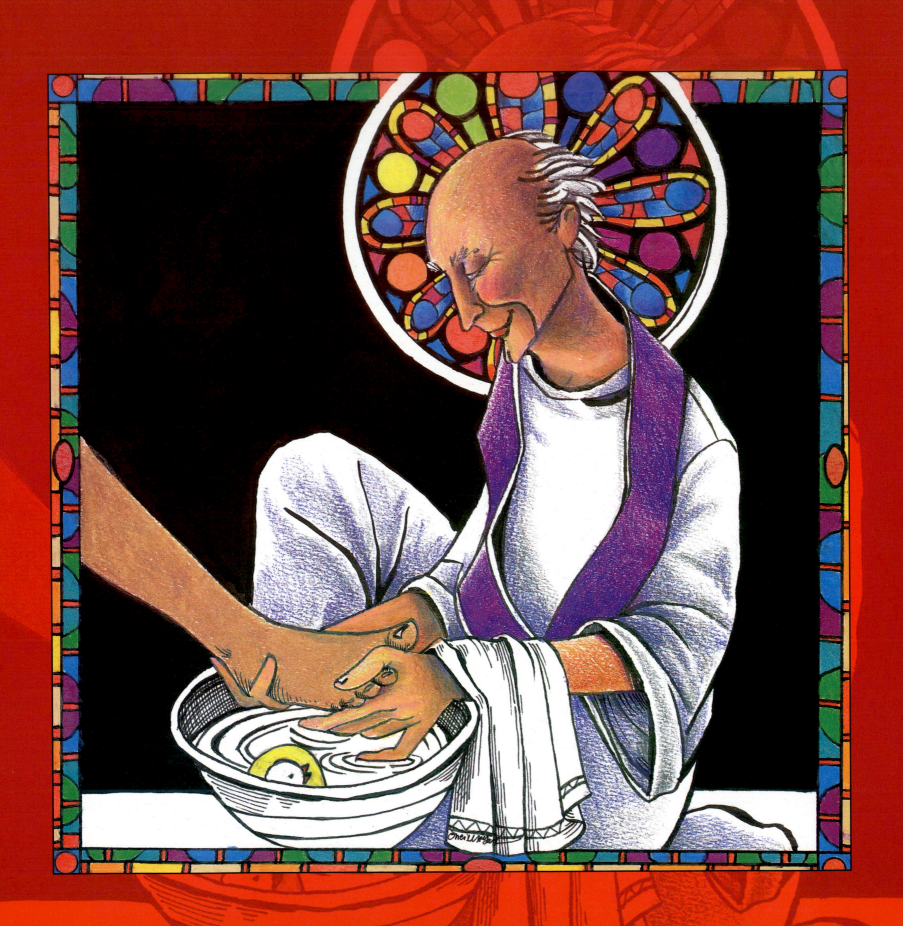

Saint John Vianney
patron of parish priests

JOHN VIANNEY, KNOWN AS "THE CURÉ OF ARS," WAS SUCH A renowned confessor that a special train line was built from Paris to Ars to accommodate the hordes of pilgrims who came to him for confession. In one year there were over 100,000 visitors! He could sit in his confessional for as many as 15 hours a day and was said to have had the ability to read souls. All this from a man whose intellectual capabilities were so simple that he barely made it through seminary! He was ordained in 1815 only because a sympathetic superior said the church needed holy priests as much as learned ones.

Jesus' example of washing his disciples' feet gives a vivid image of the vocation of the priest. Here John's purple stole reminds us of his great gifts as a confessor. His halo and border recall the stained glass windows of a parish church. This portrait is derived from actual pictures of John Vianney, whose face showed both the warmth of a kind heart and the wear of a long, difficult life. He smiles as he performs this most humble of ministries, aware that no matter whose foot he holds, it is the foot of Christ.

Saint John Vianney's feast is August 4.

"You a priest?" the young man yelled across the aisle of the crowded subway car. "I've never seen a Black priest before," he continued. The young man knew that colors and attire represent the gang, the crew or the social group on the street. Yet priesthood is more than a black suit and a Roman collar.

"Priesthood is a way of being, more than a job or a career," my bishop reminded me before he ordained me. To be a priest means to place one's charisms at the service of the community, so that the gifts of the people and the charism of the community might emerge. To be a priest is to be related to others as pastor, confessor, brother, son, father and friend. To be a priest is to be ordained, anointed and appointed for the mission of Jesus Christ—to proclaim the year of the Lord's favor, to bring good news to the poor, liberty to captives, recovery of sight to the blind and freedom to the oppressed. This is the mission statement of all Christians, and one the priest must model.

Daily interruptions are the heart of the ministry of the priest. An anxious, pregnant college student, a despairing addict, an inconsolable widower or a dying friend (all before 6:30 AM Mass) are all occasions of grace, doorways to divine intervention. And ministry is always reciprocal; the wounded healer receives and shares life. Many risks come with the territory—the savior complex, burnout, cynicism and a loss of heart.

Perhaps the greatest danger is to succumb to the immense power and privilege the priesthood brings. If this two-edged sword is not beaten into a plowshare of humble service, the ministry is corrupted. If at eucharist, the greatest exercise of priestly power, priest and people are not broken and poured out for others, then the power of the moment is weakened. This is what makes the life of Saint John Vianney so remarkable. His life was poured out completely for others—at Mass, in long hours in the confessional, and in the embrace of the sinner, the alienated and the untouchable.

"Yes," I called out to the young man in the subway, "I am a priest by the grace of God."

—Reverend Raymond G. East

Saint Joseph
patron of carpenters

HUSBAND OF MARY, FATHER OF JESUS: JOSEPH LANGUISHED FOR centuries in the early church without an identity of his own. If he was shown at all in art, he was depicted as an old man on the fringes of Jesus' nativity, a necessary but minor member of the Holy Family. That changed when Renaissance painters gave him more coverage. Saint Teresa of Avila was the first to popularize devotion to him. Joseph is revered for his obedience to the Spirit's guidance and his faithfulness and devotion to his family.

Joseph is also recognized as a laborer, a blue-collar saint. He understands the worries of the worker. Tradition also tells us that he died in the presence of Jesus and Mary, and therefore is the patron of a happy death.

Saint Joseph is at work in his woodshop, putting the finishing touches on the cradle he has to finish by December 25 (see the calendar!). The Holy Spirit is testing it out. Like all artisans, Joseph knows the sense of the sublime that comes with being engaged in a creative project. Working with our hands is a form of prayer and meditation. Joseph's workshop is an oratory, a place to discover God in the centering moments of creative expression.

Saint Joseph's feast is March 19.

I grew up around the carpentry trade, since my grandpa, dad and uncle were part of a construction business that began with my great-grandfather, who emigrated from Germany. Old barns and clubhouses were a part of my life as a boy on a small St. Louis County, Missouri, farm, and at 19 I hitchhiked my way to Alaska and did carpentry alongside an ex-convict named Big John!

Being a carpenter today is much different than it was just 50 years ago. Building methods and materials have changed significantly, and new techniques have done away with many of the age-old skills. But people still need a roof over their heads and a table at which to eat. Over the past 15 years, I have made tables and chairs for family meals, rocking chairs to lull babies to sleep, arks for the Torah and altars and communion tables for places of worship.

Carpentry provides the opportunity to work with natural materials. The challenge to use these materials with care and respect is very rewarding. The tree, like other living plants, provides us with the air we need to live. The carpenter must responsibly harvest and use the wood.

Being able to use my eyes, heart and hands to build things that will be used for generations to come gives me great satisfaction. To create an everyday object and give it beauty, warmth and soul— this is the woodworker's job.

—Martin Raterman

Saint Lawrence
patron of cooks

LAWRENCE WAS DEACON TO POPE SIXTUS II. AS SUCH HE WAS responsible for the treasury and used its resources to help the poor. He was also the Vatican librarian. After Sixtus was martyred in 258, the emperor demanded that Lawrence give him all the treasures of the church. Lawrence presented him with what he felt were the real treasures—the poor, the widowed, the sick and disabled. The emperor, failing to see the point, had Lawrence killed by slowly grilling him over an open flame.

Lawrence stands in a modern kitchen, the kind we see on cooking shows, surrounded by culinary treasures. His apron is emblazoned with his famous last words, "Turn me over, I'm done on this side!" His red kerchief is a symbol of martyrdom. The grill, his halo, is his traditional symbol in art, signifying the instrument of torture by which he died. To his right is an exhaust fan in the shape of a cross, another means of death made glorious. The cookbooks on the shelf remind us of Lawrence's role as librarian, a career for which he is also patron.

Lawrence clearly enjoys the moment of transforming raw food into a meal. Lawrence takes the most ordinary of ingredients and makes of them something memorable. Common meals become sacraments when they are made in devotion and shared with others in love.

Saint Lawrence's feast is August 10.

In one way or another, all people are interested in and need food. My own interest in cooking developed when I was young and watched my mother and grandmother prepare delicious homemade meals for the family.

Years later, when I first entered monastic life, I was assigned as apprentice to the older monk-chef. My main duties were to clean and peel the vegetables we gathered from the monastery garden, épulcher les légumes we used to call it.

From time to time the older monk-chef would allow me to prepare the soup of the day. Preparing large quantities of soup was quite an adventure. We didn't have refrigerators. Another young monk and I had to look around to see what was available in the monastery. If it was winter, fresh vegetables were scarce. We would go to the cellar to see what survived from the autumn harvest. Usually onions and potatoes became the soup base, and we would add carrots, turnips, and always beans, peas or lentils. After adding minced garlic or fresh cloves, salt and pepper, we would watch until the soup achieved the desired consistency. Then the older chef would take a taste! He was usually very understanding, reminding us that cooking required patience, experience and creativity.

Over the years I have learned that cooking is an act of cooperating with the Creator. And, as Teresa of Avila told her Carmelite sisters, "Hijas, entre los pucheros se encuentra el Señor" ("Daughters, we find the Lord among the soup of the poor").

—Brother Victor-Antoine d'Avila-Latourrette

Saint Louise de Marillac
patron of social workers

"YOUR CONVENT WILL BE THE HOUSE OF THE SICK . . . YOUR cloister the streets of the city or the wards of the hospital . . ." Supported by these words from her friend and confessor, Saint Vincent de Paul, Louise de Marillac, a widowed noblewoman and mother of one son, founded the Daughters of Charity in 1633. As a community of women, they set out to minister outside the cloister walls to the poor and sick—something very radical in their day.

Louise focused on opening soup kitchens, hospitals, orphanages and schools throughout France. She told her sisters, "Be diligent in serving the poor. Love the poor, honor them, my children, as you would honor Christ himself." Despite poor health and a demanding schedule of travel and administrative duties, Louise never lost her cheerful demeanor.

Here, Louise makes a home visit to a poor, elderly woman who is a bit hesitant about opening the door. The ripped screen, her halo, suggests the headpieces worn by the Daughters of Charity after her time. (It earned them the nickname "God's geese"!) The two crosses in the lower border symbolize our faith, the cornerstone of all Christian homes.

Saint Louise de Marillac's feast is March 15.

When I was a parish priest in a poor section of Brooklyn, New York, people came to me with their problems. Many times the problem was not one related to their faith: They were looking for food, shelter or money to pay bills. They came because they were struggling with problems that caused anxiety or depression, or that threatened the well-being of their families. Usually I had to refer them somewhere else. This frustrated them, and me as well. Often, they had already been turned away elsewhere.

Eventually, I went back to school for a social work degree. As a social worker I have served a variety of populations, usually those that are ostracized or forgotten. This has included persons with mental illness and AIDS, and most recently the elderly.

Part of my work is advocacy. I often need to intercede on behalf of clients with government agencies. This means I need to be aware of legislation that affects the poor and underserved, and I need to have a prophetic voice to speak out for the oppressed.

It has long been a part of our Christian tradition to carry out works of mercy. We are called to feed the hungry, clothe the naked, visit the sick and imprisoned, and welcome strangers. And we do all of this in the spirit of Christ, the first Christian social worker.

—Reverend Thomas Bertone, CSC

Saint Luke
patron of artists

Saint Catherine of Bologna
patron of painters

WITH AN ARTIST'S EYE FOR DETAIL, LUKE WRITES MORE THAN any other gospel writer about Christ's infancy. In the Middle Ages, people believed that Luke had not only painted a popular icon of the Madonna and Child, but that Mary and Jesus had posed for it! For that reason, Luke became patron of artists, doing double duty as patron of physicians. All the medieval art guilds operated under his patronage.

Surrounded by a border of the color spectrum, Luke works on his holy icon, sharing his halo with that of the unseen Madonna. He is bathed in the divine glow of these sacred subjects. Over his sweatshirt of martyr red, Luke's apron is splattered with green and purple paint, the mystical-liturgical colors of the church. His companion here is Catherine of Bologna, Italy, another patron of painters. Catherine created beautiful illuminated manuscripts during the Renaissance. She works with charcoal on a picture of the moon, symbol of feminine wisdom and light. Thus, her "halo" counterbalances the sunny golden disk of Luke, creating a union of complementary forces—as artists love to express!

Artists give physical form to their visions. It is their vocation to take their experience of God and paint, draw, sculpt, print or photograph it into a work of art that moves the human spirit.

It doesn't really matter if Jesus and Mary actually posed for Luke or not. There is another truth here: The God of love is incarnate in our lives, and each of us must take these raw materials and create of ourselves a masterpiece for God.

Saint Luke's feast is October 18.
Saint Catherine of Bologna's feast is March 9.

One of the middle children in a family of six, I grew up in a small house in Philadelphia, Pennsylvania. Drawing was always a part of my life. As far back as I can remember, I enjoyed putting marks on paper to tell a story or express an idea. Drawing also gave me a way of creating my own space, quiet time and sense of self. Where this need to interpret what I saw, felt and imagined came from, I am not certain, yet it is part of the magic that is inherent in my creative process.

Learning to see, as well as developing one's talent, is the cornerstone for any creative person. I observe nature and am awed by what I see. I notice people and am fascinated. It is these feelings, as well as my love of drawing and painting, that I listen to when I work. They inspire in me a need to create pictures.

Making art also has a learning curve. I gain considerable knowledge through studying and responding to an object. The continuing exercise of observation, even after years of hard work, is rewarding.

I've heard it said that art is a mirror held up for people to see how beautiful and complex our world is. I firmly believe that, and so apply brush to paper with great respect and reverence for the process.

—Jerry Pinkney

Saint Margaret of Clitherow
patron of businesswomen

MARGARET WAS THE BELOVED WIFE OF JOHN CLITHEROW, THE proprietor of a prosperous butcher shop in Elizabethan England. Margaret worked in the shop with her husband, and her skill contributed to its success. Margaret converted to Catholicism during a time in English history when the practice of Catholicism was strictly forbidden. Although not a Catholic himself, her husband did not interfere with her public expression of her faith or with her hiding priests who secretly celebrated Mass in their home.

Margaret was arrested for her actions and spent two years in prison. When she was martyred, her husband cried in anguish that they had murdered the "best wife within the kingdom and the best Catholic."

Margaret's red dress and cross convey her martyrdom. As her husband's partner in the business, she has the umbrella of his lunch wagon parked behind her as her halo. Margaret is busy on her cellular phone while she eats lunch on a city park bench. It is possible to work in the world of business and commerce and still be mindful of God's presence in our midst. No matter how busy we are with phone, fax, email and appointments, we may discover a wonderful surprise: God is by our side, and the Holy Spirit is among the pigeons!

Saint Margaret of Clitherow's feast is March 26.

I launched my own publishing company—publishing Business Ethics magazine—14 years ago because I wanted to make a difference in the world. I was a young associate publisher at the time, and I saw a trend toward greater social responsibility in practices like employee ownership, environmental stewardship and good community relations. I wanted to help that trend blossom. Creating a magazine to share information among business people seemed to be the best way I could contribute. So I quit my job and with my best friend launched Business Ethics.

It's the best decision I've ever made. Helping to make business more responsible is my life's work—which is very different from having a job. It's a mission. If I had all the money I needed and all my time was free, I would still do what I do.

Business is the best place to make a difference in the world because business is the most powerful institution on the planet. As a business owner, I understand the importance of money. But it's a mistake to think—as many business-people do—that money or profit is the only thing that matters. As publishing executive Jim Autry once said, "Profit is like breathing. You need it, but it's not what you live for."

What I live for and what my business is about is making the world a better place. We also, by the way, make a nice profit. When you look at the lives of the saints, you see their work often brought them suffering and pain. I respect and revere them. But they lived at a time when life was much harder. It's possible today to do good work in the world and still be financially comfortable.

—Marjorie Kelly

Saint Martin de Porres

patron of hairdressers

WHEN HE WAS A CHILD, MARTIN AND HIS MOTHER, A FREE Black woman named Anna, lived in extreme poverty in Lima, Peru. His father, a Spanish knight, felt that Martin's skin was too dark and abandoned him.

By the time he entered the Dominicans as a young teen, Martin had apprenticed as a barber and hairdresser, a job that also included the healing arts of surgery and pharmaceuticals in the late sixteenth century, when Martin lived. Not only could Martin cut hair, he was renowned for his healing touch.

Martin visited the poorest of the poor, the native people, and had special affection for the slaves who were brought in great numbers from Africa. He planted fruit trees along the roadside to increase the availability of food for the poor.

Martin was also known for his care and concern for animals. He once bargained with the mice who were chewing up the vestments in the sacristy, promising to keep them well fed if they would move outside. They promptly agreed.

There's a mouse in this beauty shop, on the counter to the right. A broom and a mouse are Saint Martin's traditional symbols in art. Martin wears a black vest because in his day Dominican brothers wore a black scapular.

Martin was a wonderworker. Through his hairdressing ministry he created beauty and helped people feel better about themselves. Even more, his touch could heal sin-sick souls and lighten the loads of heavy hearts. He is also known as patron of those who work for social and interracial justice.

Saint Martin de Porres's feast is November 3.

How very lucky we hairdressers are! Our job makes people happy. They come to us, look into our mirrors, and with our help begin to see themselves as beautiful. Suddenly, their faces radiate a new confidence. I receive such energy back when I make others happy about themselves. It's immediate gratification from my job.

But what really causes such positive responses? Certainly our talents contribute. To express our talents, however, we rely on the power of touch. Think about it. How many professions will actually allow you to touch a stranger with kindness? Touch is a powerful conduit for the spirit, connecting people together and facilitating healing. When we feel connected to someone we somehow feel enriched. Maybe our forebears were on target when they asked the barber to be the surgeon.

We hairdressers also never work in isolation. We meet people from all walks of life. Knowing them enhances our lives, sometimes for many, many years. It is an honor to be in a profession that allows me to participate in such personal transformation, and it rewards me by broadening my world through the experiences of others.

—Maxine Kroll

Saint Mary Magdalene
patron of perfumers

ACCORDING TO THE GOSPELS OF MARK, MATTHEW AND JOHN, Mary of Magdala went to Jesus' burial place to anoint his body with myrrh. She was the first to discover the empty tomb and the first to announce the resurrection to his disciples. Thus, she has been called the apostle to the apostles and the patron of preachers.

A popular French legend says that after Christ's ascension, Mary Magdalene, along with Martha and Lazarus, sailed to southern France, where they spent the rest of their lives preaching to the people there. Perhaps Mary Magdalene brought a jar of myrrh with her and got their world-famous perfume industry off the ground!

Behind her head we see the lights of the rising sun in a tomb-shaped mirror, because Mary had gone to Jesus' tomb to anoint his body. Her traditional symbol in art is an alabaster jar of perfume. In the display case are gift boxes arranged to remind us of Calvary. They are wrapped with bows to suggest little crosses, reminding us that Mary Magdalene, one of Jesus' few loyal friends, stood beneath his cross as he died. On the lower right we see a pair of feet—are these Jesus' feet, which legend tells us that Mary washed?

Like Mary Magdalene, we must take the stories of our lives and lay them at the foot of the cross. There we discover the good news of salvation, a healing perfume for our weary souls.

Saint Mary Magdalene's feast is July 22.

Perfumery is one of the many crafts practiced at the Abbey of Regina Laudis. This follows the tradition preserved by Saint Benedict in his Rule, chapter 57: "If there be crafts-people in the monastery, let them practice their crafts with all humility, provided the abbot gives them permission."

As a chemist, I am able to use my professional training in a practical, rewarding way through the preparation of perfume, a work that encompasses all the seasons of the year. The abbey's summer gardens provide the idea for a specific scent. Winter months are used to study the elements of its composition. Blending of the essences comes in early spring. The new fragrance matures into a full-bodied perfume throughout the summer and is finally ready for packaging in the fall. Then I have the joy of working with others to present the perfume, along with other natural beauty products and herbs for cooking, among the exquisite weavings, pottery, candles and stained glass ornaments at our Monastic Art Shop throughout the year.

The ultimate perfume I prepare, with a deep sense of reverence and prayer, is the "Cecilia Chrism Fragrance," which elevates perfume to a higher dimension. The bishop mixes this fragrance with olive oil, consecrates it as chrism, and sends it out to his parishes so that newly baptized babies may be anointed and others may be confirmed.

Chrism smells beautiful, and this smell is a sign of God's grace in the sacraments, leading us to ponder the invisible mysteries of our salvation. The bishop also uses chrism to consecrate the altar of a new church. It is with faith and loving service that I participate in making this precious oil, used in the sacramental life of the church. In one of his letters, Saint Athanasius, a fourth-century bishop of Alexandria, says that "chrism has the fragrance and odor of him who anoints, and those who are anointed say, 'We are the fragrance of Christ' (2 Corinthians 2:15)."

—*Sister Catherine of Alexandria, OSB*

Saint Matthew
patron of bankers and accountants

IN JESUS' DAY, TAX COLLECTORS SUCH AS MATTHEW WERE social outcasts, considered the lowest of the low on the career ladder. They took money from the poor and gave it to the Roman conquerors. Yet Jesus befriended and even ate dinner with tax collectors! He called Matthew, a tax collector, to life as an apostle.

Green details from dollar bills and coins fill the border around Saint Matthew. He is lost in thought, safely ensconced behind the teller's window. The open door of the empty vault behind him tells us that his true treasures lie elsewhere. Everything that is most important in his world sits before him on his desk. Front and center is the illuminated banker's lamp reminding us of the light of Christ. His Bible is open to the gospel of Matthew and his pen is uncapped, ready to write.

In order to emphasize the human nature of Jesus, Matthew's gospel begins with a long, detailed list of Christ's ancestors. How like an accountant! We need men and women to work with details and crunch numbers. They keep track of our gains and losses, help us buy homes and send children to school. Saint Matthew reminds us that all are called to follow Christ, and all are welcome at his table.

Saint Matthew's feast is September 21.

Some say that money is the root of all evil. Not so. All things are good when used according to the will of God.

Community banking is an integral part of helping families care for the fruits of their labor. Families entrust us with their life savings. Their hard-earned dollars are soon withdrawn to pay bills.

I chose to work in banking because it is a way to help people be good stewards of their financial resources. Most of us need to learn this skill, and it is my job to provide financial educational programs to families in our communities. We also sponsor services as simple as helping new parents open a savings account for their child or wire money to other parts of the world.

The dream of many of our account holders is to buy their first home. We provide seminars for first-time homebuyers and family credit counseling. In these I get to know individual families, their children, and any specific needs they might have. In an era in which many financial institutions are driven by profit, community banking strives to look out for the family's interests and protect the family from being financially overextended.

Banking is about much more than money. It is about developing livable communities and neighborhoods, and helping individuals be responsible with what God has given them.

—Matthew M. Brophy

Saint Michael the Archangel
patron of police

SAINT MICHAEL THE ARCHANGEL IS THE ORIGINAL ACTION hero of art. With cape and wings and hair billowing around him, he is traditionally shown chasing the devil out of heaven. Amidst the smoke and lightning bolts, an evil-looking serpent with red eyes and fangs writhes in pain beneath the thrust of Michael's golden spear. Michael is strong and valiant, the head of God's army protecting earth from evil forces. No wonder he was immensely popular in the Middle Ages as the guardian of fortresses and coastline borders.

Police are called to serve and protect the community. They willingly place themselves in dangerous situations, yet they must use their power with authority and restraint. No wonder Michael is still invoked today as the patron of police and all those who keep us from harm.

We are presented here with a peaceful Saint Michael. Mounted on his mighty steed, his scarf blowing in the wind, Michael keeps the world safe at a Thanksgiving Day parade. Coffee in hand, he goes eye to eye with the devil, a harmless balloon, tethered and full of hot air, that passes over the pointed steeple of the church. The primary comic-book colors of an action hero fill the border of zigzags and balloon strings.

Saint Michael the Archangel's feast is September 29.

I was almost certain when I began college that I wanted to be a police officer. I knew that every day there were battles being waged for justice, and I wanted to be a part of a noble and honorable profession that protects the rights of those who sometimes cannot protect themselves. I hoped to be the kind of police officer who would take the risks that come with preserving the safety of the community.

Being a police officer is about being a servant to the community. It is about managing the authority that the community bestows on you when you take your oath before them and God. Police provide a security that allows people to live more fully. A community needs to know that someone is working day and night to keep the place safe, to be available in emergencies and to help people through difficult situations.

The struggle for justice is rarely easy. After many years of police work, I probably work harder than ever to preserve the safety of the community. I also know in my mind and heart that this profession has rewarded me with the opportunity to touch the lives of many wonderful people and to help our community flourish.

—Frank Kaminski

Saint Peter

patron of fishermen and fisherwomen

AS CHILDREN SOME OF US WERE TOLD THAT PETER CRIED SO much over denying Jesus that his tears made ruts in his cheeks. This sensitive outpouring of emotion hardly fits the popular image we have of a rough and tough fisherman with callused hands and a face weatherbeaten by salty air. But Peter knew a good storm when he saw one, both the kind that churns the waters and the kind that rages within us. He's also the one who fell into the water after walking on it, who said he'd never deny Christ but proceeded to do so three times, who wanted to construct booths at the transfiguration. This ordinary man is the last one we'd consider to be the first leader of those who follow Jesus, but God is full of surprises!

Peter says grace before eating a breakfast of fried fish. With the key to the kingdom around his neck, perhaps he reflects on how to "feed my sheep," Jesus' command before he ascended into heaven. Peter's hat is covered with lures, a symbol of the many souls he lured to God. The curtains are made of fishnet, since Peter is also the patron saint of net-makers. He did drop his nets that fateful day on the beach, when he gave up the call of the sea to follow Jesus.

Saint Peter's feast is June 29.

Being a fisherman is a special calling. After all, Christ chose fishermen to be his "fishers of men." The ocean is a formidable foe, so the challenge of making one's living from the sea requires a love of the sea, a strong back, a knowledge of the tides and the stars (as a navigational aid), and a deep faith in God. Being on a fishing boat with miles of ocean surrounding the boat and only the stars above fills one with awe and respect for the elements of nature.

My family has been fishing for centuries—first in Sicily and, since 1895, in San Francisco, San Diego and San Pedro, California. Commercial fishing requires many skills. First, one must know how to navigate and locate schools of fish. The seasons and the moon play an important part. Dangers abound in storms at sea, yet all the fishermen I grew up around and worked with seemed to love being at one with the sea, with God to guide them. Nearly all fishermen are religious. Many fishing boats have chapels, especially those venturing from California ports down to Mexican and South American waters. Many boats are named for patron saints, and the blessing of a fishing boat is as important as the construction. In the past there were annual blessings of the fishing fleet, as God's presence is vital to the lives of fishermen.

—Nicholas Giacalone

Saint Sebastian
patron of athletes

SEBASTIAN LIVED DURING THE REIGN OF THE ROMAN EMPEROR
Diocletian, a fierce persecutor of Christians. Sebastian became
a soldier for one reason—so he could sneak messages in and
out of prison to the captured Christians. After being promoted
to captain of the guard, Sebastian was caught and martyred. He
was shot through with arrows, but survived with the help of
Saint Irene, who nursed him back to health. The traditional
depiction of Sebastian tied to a pillar with arrows piercing him
led to his being considered the patron of archers. Because he
was always shown in fine physical shape, Sebastian also
became popular as the patron of all athletes.

Sebastian plays a game of soccer in a crowded stadium, a
setting that recalls the arenas where so many early Christians
were martyred. It is night to remind us of the secrecy so central
to his life as a Christian. There are two emblems on his uniform
of martyr red: the arrow, his traditional symbol in art; and the
Holy Spirit, a badge he wears with honor. Instead of the usual
advertisements, the spectator stands are decorated with flags
from around the world. Soccer is a universally loved sport, and
like any sport played well, can teach us something about the
health and the beauty of human nature when mind, body and
spirit work together.

Saint Sebastian's feast is January 20.

*I never had any intention of becoming a coach; I had plans
to become a lawyer. As the good Lord would have it, a simple
phone call from my uncle changed the course of my life. He
wondered if I knew anyone who knew baseball and could
teach this sport to a group of boys. I immediately volunteered
my friend, Tommy Clark. Little did I realize Tommy's silent
ambition was to sell my attributes to the Mother Superior,
Sister Batilde. The rest, as they say, is history. When we
walked away, I had a job I don't recall applying for or accept-
ing. Our first season ended with no wins and 16 losses. And
my life was forever changed as I soon realized that significant
victories had been won off the field.*

*I find great fulfillment in my profession of coaching:
the thrill of competition, teaching kids when they're most
impressionable, and the opportunity to touch lives. Sports is
an excellent vehicle through which to help develop a young
person's spiritual life. Show me someone with a spiritual
commitment, and I'll also see a better person.*

*Sports is also an excellent medium through which to
encourage proper priorities, discipline, teamwork and
cooperation. All of these characteristics are essential to the
creation of good, well-rounded individuals. All of my players
understand the importance of priorities and adhering to
them. In order, these are God, family, school, basketball. We
must use basketball and not allow basketball to use us. As
Knute Rockne so aptly put it, "I have to wait to see what
kind of people they've become. Then one can ask me what I
think about the impact that I had on their lives." The ability
to touch—even change—another's life is both confounding
and inspiring to me.*

*John R. Wooden, coach emeritus of UCLA,
sums up my advice to anyone in any profession at any stage of their lives: "Learn as
if you will live forever; live as if you will
die tomorrow." What more is there to say?*

—Morgan Wootton

Saint Thérèse of Lisieux
patron of airplane pilots

Saint Joseph of Cupertino
patron of air travelers

FROM THE TIME SHE WAS 16 UNTIL HER DEATH ON SEPTEMBER 30, 1897, at the age of 24, Thérèse Martin never left her small cloistered monastery in Normandy, France. Prior to that, while on pilgrimage to Rome, she got her first ride in an elevator, probably the closest she ever got to flying. So why did Pope Pius XII declare Thérèse patron of pilots? Because she traveled the world in her heart.

Thérèse had a burning desire to move to a Carmelite monastery in Vietnam, and she maintained a special affection for foreign missions. Before she died, she promised she would spend her time in heaven doing good on earth, and to prove it she'd shower the world with roses from heaven.

The face of Thérèse in this drawing is derived from an actual photograph of her. On the flight with her is Saint Joseph of Cupertino, reading a floating book. He was a seventeenth-century mystic who enjoyed the gift of levitation. Because he could bilocate, he occupies two seats on the plane!

Saint Thérèse once said she was more like the sparrow, who could reach only humble heights, than the majestic eagle, who soared so high. Her spirituality is called the "Little Way" and teaches that each of us, whether a sparrow or an eagle, a Piper Cub or a supersonic jet, has a mission on earth.

Saint Thérèse of Lisieux's feast is October 1.
Saint Joseph of Cupertino's feast is September 18.

When asked to write this piece, I just happened to be reading The Story of a Soul, *the autobiography of Thérèse of Lisieux, patron of airplane pilots. I had not known that she was one of our patrons until then. After reading the book I'm very happy that she is.*

Why Thérèse, also known as the Little Flower, was chosen as patron of pilots is not readily apparent. Our lives and hers can be very similar though. She was forced by her calling as a cloistered nun to live apart from her family. Pilots are forced to be away from their families for training purposes or flight schedules. As Thérèse came to love her family more in the separation, we have the opportunity to do the same. Being a pilot also gives the opportunity to bring families together across great distances.

Thérèse had a great interest in the missions. As a cloistered nun she could not leave her monastery, so she wrote letters and sent prayers around the world. The Little Flower, through her "Little Way," became a powerful intercessor for the salvation of souls. She learned in her simplicity that love, prayer and obedience are powerful ways to love Jesus and Mary.

As pilots traveling to many cities around the world, we have the chance to meet all kinds of people who need our prayers and loving charity. We also have the opportunity to seek out churches and other places to share prayer and the Mass with God's children from every corner of the globe.

—*James L. Daro*

Saint Thomas More
patron of lawyers

Saint Catherine of Alexandria
patron of jurors

Saint Ivo of Kermartin
patron of judges

THOMAS MORE, CHANCELLOR OF ENGLAND UNDER KING HENRY VIII, was the noblest of lawyers who literally gave his life in defense of the truth as he saw it. A brilliant and respected statesman, More did his best to serve the king. When he could not assent to King Henry's repudiation of the Catholic church's authority, More resigned his post and retired to the country. He spoke eloquently on the importance of following one's conscience, and he sought to remain silent rather than speak against the king. His silence, however, spoke even more loudly, and his refusal to sign an oath disavowing the pope's authority over the king led to his imprisonment and death.

This drawing is based on Hans Holbein's famous portrait of Thomas More. While not wearing the velvet cloak seen in the original, Thomas still wears the medallion of his office of chancellor. His red bow tie and handkerchief symbolize his martyrdom by beheading. Saint Catherine of Alexandria stands in the jury box with the Holy Spirit. According to legend, she possessed noteworthy debating skills and thus is the patron of jurors and philosophers. Saint Ivo of Kermartin, whose name appears on the plaque of the judge's bench, is the patron saint of judges.

Saint Thomas More's feast is June 22.
Saint Catherine of Alexandria's feast is November 25.
Saint Ivo of Kermartin's feast is May 19.

The practice of law—which should and can be about justice—is an exciting, creative way to assist others. In my legal career I have prosecuted criminals and defended people charged with crimes. I have worked as a Peace Corps volunteer in a justice system in Somalia, Africa, and argued at every level of state and federal courts, including the United States Supreme Court, on behalf of disabled and underprivileged persons.

As public guardian, I have represented children who have been abused by their parents or foster parents and acted to protect the interests of elderly people who are disabled by Alzheimer's disease or other age-related illnesses. I have also supervised a staff of attorneys and social workers who work with and for these people.

My clients have included an elderly man who served in both World Wars, had saved $100,000, and was swindled out of his life savings by an unscrupulous individual. Helping the elderly and children negotiate the court system is one of the greatest privileges a lawyer can have. Helping people obtain justice is a satisfying and good way to use one's talents on behalf of others.

—*Patrick T. Murphy*

55

about the contributors

Reverend Thomas Bertone works with the elderly and infirm members of his community, the Congregation of the Holy Cross. He received his Master of Social Work degree from Catholic University of America in Washington, D.C., and has been active in social justice education and advocacy.

Sister Laurie Brink, a Dominican Sister of Sinsinawa, is a doctoral student in biblical studies at the University of Chicago Divinity School. She has taught at Dominican University, River Forest, Illinois. During the summers she works in archeology at Caesarea Maritima, Israel.

Matthew M. Brophy is a community development officer for Second Federal Savings and Loan, a bank that primarily serves the Latino community in the Chicago area. He holds a Master of Divinity from Catholic Theological Union in Chicago.

Dave Brubeck is a world-renowned pianist, composer and conductor. The Dave Brubeck Quartet was responsible for the resurgence of jazz in the 1950s and '60s. Their album *Time Out* was the first record to sell one million copies. In 1994 President Clinton presented Dave Brubeck with the National Medal of the Arts.

Sister Catherine of Alexandria, a Benedictine nun of the Abbey of Regina Laudis, Bethlehem, Connecticut, has degrees in chemistry from the Catholic University of America and the University of Sheffield, England. Her duties at the abbey include care of the herb gardens and the preparation of herbal and beauty products. She is also the manager of the Monastic Art Shop.

James L. Daro, a captain for American Airlines, was born, raised and still lives in small-town Nebraska. He has been married for 31 years and has eight children and ten grandchildren. He lives in Garrison, Nebraska, population 78, and has no plans to leave anytime soon.

Brother Victor-Antoine d'Avila-Latourrette is a monk of Our Lady of the Resurrection Monastery in LaGrangeville, New York. He is the author of *Fresh from the Monastery Garden, From a Monastery Kitchen* and *Twelve Months of Monastery Soups*.

Tesse Hartigan Donnelly is the mother of five grown children. She is a founding member of the Saint Giles Family Mass Community in Oak Park, Illinois, where she and her husband are active members of the adult learning committee.

Reverend Raymond G. East is pastor of the Church of the Nativity in Washington, D.C.

Thomas C. Fox is publisher of the Kansas City–based *National Catholic Reporter,* a Catholic newsweekly.

Nicholas Giacalone was nine when he started fishing with his father during school vacations. His grandfather, a Sicilian fisherman, immigrated to the United States in 1895, and the tradition of fishing has been carried on in the family ever since. Nicholas and his wife volunteer for the Apostleship of the Sea Catholic Maritime Ministry in San Pedro, California.

Therese Maguire Hester owns Garland Florists in Oak Park, Illinois. She is married and the mother of two children.

Edward L. Jeep is a captain in the United States Marine Corps and is stationed in San Diego, California. He flies the CH-46E helicopter.

Jack Jezreel divides his time between agriculture and social justice education. He and his family live in Kentucky, where they have grown vegetables for the last 12 years.

Frank Kaminski, chief of police for the city of Evanston, Illinois, has promoted partnership programs between the police department and community groups to aid in crime prevention.

Sister Carol Keehan, president of Providence Hospital in Washington, D.C., is a Daughter of Charity of Saint Vincent de Paul. She is also a nurse, has advanced degrees in health care finance, and has been a vice president for nursing and CEO of two hospitals.

Marjorie Kelly is cofounder and publisher of *Business Ethics: Corporate Social Responsibility Report*. She lives in Minneapolis, Minnesota.

Christine Kenny-Sheputis left a career in fundraising to follow her desire to someday open a tearoom. She manages a bakery and cafe in a Chicago suburb.

Maxine Kroll owns and operates Maxine's, a beauty salon in Chicago, Illinois.

Theresa Kubasak has taught the early grades primarily in public schools for over 25 years. She is on the staff at National Louis University, where she teaches in the demonstration school.

Patrick T. Murphy is Cook County Public Guardian, Chicago, Illinois. He has been an outspoken advocate for children and is the author of *Wasted: The Plight of America's Unwanted Children*.

Jerry Pinkney has illustrated more than 75 children's books and has received three Caldecott Honor Medals, four Coretta Scott King Awards, and two King Honors. His interest in different cultures, especially African American culture, has inspired much of his work.

Jean Quashnock is associate professor of physics at Carthage College, Kenosha, Wisconsin. His research interests include cosmology, large-scale structure in the universe, gamma-ray bursts and quasars.

Martin Raterman, a fourth-generation carpenter, works in black walnut, cherry, oak and maple. His handmade furniture can be found in private homes, places of worship, restaurants and boardrooms throughout the United States. He lives in Missouri.

Fred Rogers is the creator and host of the television program *Mr. Rogers' Neighborhood*. Now in its thirtieth year, the program continues to delight and educate children and adults. He is also an ordained Presbyterian minister.

Sister Mary Luke Tobin has been a Sister of Loretto for over 70 years. She was the first American woman auditor at the Second Vatican Council and has been active in peace and justice ministries.

Janice Vascott of Santa Fe, New Mexico, has been an architect for 20 years. Her special interest is the use of alternative, environmentally sustainable materials, such as straw bale, and solar energy. In addition to designing residential housing, she has been involved with the straw bale project at Christ in the Desert Monastery, Abiquiu, New Mexico.

Morgan Wootton has been a teacher and coach at DeMatha Catholic High School for the past 44 years. He is the "winning-est" high school basketball coach in the history of the game. Among his numerous honors is his induction into the Basketball Hall of Fame.

about the artist

Brother Michael (Mickey) O'Neill McGrath is an Oblate of Saint Francis de Sales in Washington, D.C., whose full-time ministry is art. In addition to creating art for most of today's leading Catholic publishers, as well as parishes nationwide, Mickey conducts retreats, workshops and parish missions centered on the relationship between art, prayer and religious faith.

Brother Mickey is currently working on two more books for this series. *Patrons and Protectors: More Occupations* will include such saints as Apollonia, patron of dentists; Gemma, patron of pharmacists; John the Baptist, patron of roadworkers; and Francis of Assisi, patron of veterinarians and zookeepers.

Patrons and Protectors: In Times of Need will highlight saints associated with particular illnesses and disasters, and will include Lucy (blindness), Camillus de Lellis (AIDS), Maximilian Kolbe (drug addiction) and Gregory the Wonderworker (floods).